ELIZABETH A. NIXON, ESQ.

Published by XP Publishing
A department of Christian Services Association
P.O. Box 1017, Maricopa, Arizona 85139
United States of America
www.XPpublishing.com

ISBN 13: 978-1-936101-25-2
ISBN 10: 1-936101-25-4

For Worldwide Distribution. Printed in Canada.

DEDICATION

This book is dedicated to my husband, Jon,
who has always believed in me,
and that has made all the difference.

TABLE OF CONTENTS

FOREWORD BY PATRICIA KING   1 1

A TEACHING ON DECREES   13

What Is a Decree?
What Does It Mean to Decree?
How to Use Decrees
Scriptural Precedent of Decrees
Getting into Alignment
Do It! Live It! Be It!

DECREES INSPIRED BY THE PSALMS

1. Psalm 1 – I Am Blessed   27
2. Psalm 2 – Heavenly Perspective   29
3. Psalm 3 – Victory!   31
4. Psalm 7 – Vindication from the Lord   33
5. Psalm 15 – Godly Character   35

6.   Psalm 23 – At Home and At Peace with the Lord   37

7.   Psalm 24 – A Decree for the Media Mountain   41

8.   Psalm 31 – How Great Is Your Goodness   45

9.   Psalm 32 – Forgiven   47

10.   Psalm 34:1-8 – I Am Yours   49

11.   Psalm 34:9 – Everything, Always   51

12.   Psalm 37 – All That I Long For   53

13.   Psalm 45 – Standing Tall   57

14.   Psalm 63:8 – Right Hand   59

15.   Psalm 65:4 – How Blessed   61

16.   Psalm 66:8-13 – Inhabit Me, Oh Lord   63

17.   Psalm 67 – His Face Shines   65

18.   Psalm 84 – Just a Glimpse of You   67

19.   Psalm 91 – Protection   69

20.   Psalm 102 – The Lord Is Before Me   71

21.   Psalm 112:1-5 – The Light of God   73

22.   Psalm 112:5-7 – A Right Attitude   77

23.   Psalm 118:24-29 – The Day the Lord Made   79

24.   Psalm 119: 32-40 – Life – God's Way   81

25.   Psalm 125 – Secure   83

26.   Psalm 127 – Rest and Provision, Even in Sleep   87

27.   Psalm 128 – Always More, Always Higher   89

28.   Psalm 144 – Life Is Good   91

29.   Psalm 145 – Bless the Lord   93

30.   Psalm 146 – Unlimited!   95

31.   Psalm 147 – His Goodness Invades   97

Decrees Inspired by the Psalmic Hebrew Language

1. Decree Inspired by the Hebrew Words: Light and Way *'owr & derek*   101
2. Decree Inspired by the Hebrew Word: To Judge *shaphat*   103
3. Decree Inspired by the Hebrew Word: Inheritance *nachalah*   105
4. Decree Inspired by the Hebrew Word: Peace *shalowm*   107
5. Decree Inspired by the Hebrew Word: Increase *yebuwl*   109

Decrees for the 7 Mountains Inspired by Psalm 24

7 Mountains, as Identified by Dr. Lance Wallnau   115
1. A Decree for the Business Mountain   117
2. A Decree for the Government Mountain   121
3. A Decree for the Family Mountain   125
4. A Decree for the Religion Mountain   129
5. A Decree for the Media Mountain   133
6. A Decree for the Education Mountain   137
7. A Decree for the Entertainment Mountain   141

FOREWORD

BY PATRICIA KING

I have always believed in the power of God-inspired procla-
mations, and I personally make decreeing the Word a daily
discipline due to the great benefits I have received from such
practice.

I remember when the Lord first spoke to me about the benefits of decrees. I was in a season where I was shut down emo-
tionally, and I lacked inspiration. He spoke a clear word to my
heart concerning the importance of making daily decrees of
the Word of God in order to fortify and edify my spirit during
that time. For months, I declared daily who I was in Christ
and what I had in Him.

Though I made bold statements based on the Scriptures, I did
not actually feel like, "I was the head and not the tail." I did not
feel like, "I was the righteousness of God in Christ Jesus." I did

not feel like, "I was more than a conqueror in Christ." Yet the Word said that I was indeed all these things.

At that time in my life, I made a quality decision to believe the Word of God more than my circumstances, more than my feelings or lack of them, and more than what any individual might say.

During the months of making daily decrees, I found things shifting in my circumstances. The Word of God truly does not return void but accomplishes everything it is sent to do. The Word of God builds frameworks in the unseen realm that then manifest in the natural. Decrees are very powerful!

Elizabeth Nixon skillfully unpacks insights regarding decrees. As a respected attorney, Elizabeth is familiar with the legal authority behind decrees. You will love some of the revelation she unfolds. Your faith will increase and you will be truly stirred to engage in proclaiming decrees of the Word. Don't be surprised if you find your life taking new turns that release greater realms of blessing and opportunity.

You will love this book. It is one you will want to keep in your library as a resource. Or put it with your Bible to use during your devotions. Be blessed as you enjoy this powerful tool. I have been.

A Teaching on Decrees

Thou shalt decree a thing,
and it shall be established unto thee:
and the light shall shine upon thy ways.
—Job 22:28 KJV—

The Word of God directs us to "decree a thing." Using God's own words in the Scriptures is a powerful way to make decrees because God's Word does not return void. It accomplishes its full purpose (Isaiah 55:11). Using Scripture is a safe way to decree, because we can be assured that we are in alignment with His heart.

WHAT IS A DECREE?

The meaning of the word *decree* is rich and full. Understanding what a decree is will radically and forever change the way you approach life. There are several aspects to the word, all of which bring energy and vitality to your life and prayer time. Get ready to be transformed!

- A decree begins with a statement of purpose, truth or vision. But the depth of the statement is much more than just an announcement.

- The authority behind the statement is the same as the authority of a law being enacted, or an order being issued by a Court.

- Added to that is the aspect that the statement being made is one and the same as the very purposes of God.

- Lastly, the impact of the decree is such that the plans and wiles of the enemy are cut off and destroyed.

WHAT DOES IT MEAN TO DECREE?

The English meaning of the word *decree* is: "an order or ruling issued with the power of the Court." A biblical meaning expands *decree* to include: "the will or purpose of God interpreted through events considered to be of His doing."

These definitions help us understand the authority behind our words when we make declarations. For example, when we make declarations regarding God's provision over our home and families, we understand that we speak those words with the same power as a Court's order and proclaiming God's purposes.

Using Scripture as the basis of our decrees increases the authority and effectiveness of the decrees. It also increases our confidence and faith. For example, you could simply decree over your home, "*God has blessed this home and we enjoy His provision.*" However, when we are battling fear or lack of faith, we can sometimes wonder if we're just making it up or speaking out words of wishful thinking. It can be easy to be defeated in your mind by the enemy.

But, when we use Bible verses, we know that we are speaking truth, which increases our faith. With increased faith and confidence, our authority also rises. For instance, the decree suggested above can be expanded and strengthened to become the following decree, which was inspired by Psalm 112 (The Message):

> *I am blessed because I fear the Lord,*
> *I cherish and relish His commandments.*
> *Because of this, my children are strong and full of integrity*
> *And my home brims with wealth!*
> *I am unfazed by rumor or gossip.*
> *My heart is ready and ever trusting in the Lord,*
> *I am forever blessed, relaxed among my enemies.*

This is such a strong statement. It has been my experience that the promises and truths in God's Word are so much more than we would ever hope to claim on our own.

The Hebrew definition of *decree* expands our understanding of the word and provides a glimpse into what happens in the supernatural realm when we make decrees. In Hebrew, *decree* means: "to divide, cut in two, to cut off, to destroy, separate or exclude."

Therefore, when we make decrees we are actually dividing and separating. We are cutting off and destroying. For example, a decree about prosperity divides and separates prosperity from lack. It cuts off lack and destroys poverty spirits.

As applied to the decree above from Psalm 112, when we say we are blessed we not only set ourselves apart for the Lord's blessing and establish it with Godly authority, we also cut off anything purposed to rob us of that blessing. When we decree, "*My children are strong and full of integrity,*" we divide their strength from weakness and set them apart from deception. When we declare their integrity, we cut off and destroy dishonesty and unrighteousness. When we declare, "*My home brims with wealth,*" not only are we decreeing wealth but we are cutting off and destroying lack and spirits of poverty.

A German word similar to the derivative of *decree* is the word *diktat*, which is also a very strong word. Its meaning is: "a statement or order that cannot be opposed." Also: "a harsh settlement imposed on a defeated opponent or enemy." Applied to our use of making decrees over our lives with the truths of God's Word, we see how fitting this definition is, because it means that our decrees cannot be opposed and are being imposed upon our defeated enemy.

So while the English definition and biblical tradition imbue us with confidence and authority about our position to speak over our lives, the Hebrew and German definitions increase it and let us see that our words themselves are actually defeating the enemy. Powerful!

How to Use Decrees

Decrees are not like the "positive affirmations" prescribed by New Age spiritualism or advocates of "The Secret" style-philosophies. Decrees are not words of wishful thinking simply said out loud. Decrees, based on scriptural truths, can do two things: renew our minds, and create a heavenly atmosphere. Both of these are very important.

RENEWING YOUR MIND:

Romans 12:2 exhorts us to renew our minds. In the Greek, this means a literal renovation, a change for the better in our intellectual ability to reason and to understand. Decrees do this for us. Remembering what *decree* means, when we declare biblical truths we cut off and destroy the lies of the enemy which pollute our minds. We mend our thoughts with the truth. And we order that truth over ourselves, our household, and our spheres of influence with the same authority that a Court Order would impose.

CREATING A HEAVENLY ATMOSPHERE:

When the Lord modeled prayer for us, He gave us the directive, "Thy (God's) Kingdom come, Thy will be done on earth, as it is in heaven" (Matthew 6:10). By this simple line, Jesus showed us that it is God's intent for us to be able to enjoy all the benefits of heaven and His Kingdom, now here on earth. Decrees, then, cause us to come into agreement with God's will and His Kingdom. As such, they are a means of creating the kind of atmosphere here on earth where His Kingdom can manifest.

SPEAKING OUT LOUD:

Finally, there is the aspect of speaking the decrees out loud. Perhaps the best example of the power of the spoken word comes from Genesis 1:3, where "God said," and it was so. In fact, this Genesis example of God decreeing, "Let there be light," is exactly what we are decreeing – we are decreeing light into our lives. In fact, the word "light" from Genesis 1:3 is translated as not only heavenly lights such as stars but also the light of life, the light of God's instruction and the light of prosperity. It is the light of God's truth, righteousness and justice. Our spoken words are decreeing the manifestation of His Kingdom come on earth as it is in heaven.

JOB 22:28

The following decree was inspired by Job 22:28. It was developed by incorporating the ancient Hebrew translations of each specific word to provide a comprehensive understanding of what is readily available to us.

Decree inspired by Job 22:28:

- I am in agreement with the will and purposes of God.

- I decree over my life and those in my household, and over my entire sphere of influence, that all the promises God has for me are mine!

- I authorize the full implementation of His promises, effective immediately. God's purposes for my life cannot be shaken or hindered.

- The light of God's life, prosperity and instruction shine upon me, they enlighten my mind and my spirit, directing my moral character and the course of my life.

SCRIPTURAL PRECEDENT OF DECREES

Using decrees is a new concept for some. Therefore, it is prudent to search the Scriptures for examples of decrees so that we may be confident in their biblical precedent. Three primary examples are available for us in the Word, all of which endorse the concept and use of decrees.

~ First, there is a record of God's decree over David, given as an ante-picture of His decree over Jesus as Messiah

~ Second is the directive from Job 22:28

~ Third is the 23rd Psalm

First, God's decree in Psalm 2:7-8 reads:

- *"I will surely tell of the decree of the Lord,*

- *He has said to Me, 'You are My Son, Today I have begotten you.*

- *Ask of Me, and I will surely give the nations as Your inheritance,*

- *And the very ends of the earth as your possession.' "*

In this verse we see that the Lord made a decree. As recorded in this Psalm, it is both an affirmation of the Lord's own (probably David) as well as a precursor for God's affirmation of Jesus as Messiah. In either case, it is a record of God making a decree. Ephesians 5:1 exhorts us to be imitators of God, so it is appropriate for us to imitate Him in making decrees.

Second, the book of Job affirms decrees in Job 22:28, which reads, "Thou shalt also decree a thing, and it shall be established unto thee." The use of the word *shall* is significant. In legal contracts, words like *may* and *shall* are used very carefully and purposefully because they have very different meanings. The use of *shall* in this verse means that we are not simply being encouraged to decree, we are being commanded to decree. This verse directly instructs us to make decrees, "thou shalt," and follows up with the result – it *shall* be established for you.

Instructions with promises attached, like this one, are excellent resources for the strengthening of our faith and obedience.

Third, the 23rd Psalm, written by David, is probably the most well-known of all the Psalms. It is written in the form of a decree. Read it anew as a decree:

+ The Lord is my Shepherd
+ I shall not want
+ He makes me lie down in green pastures
+ He leads me beside quiet waters
+ He restores my soul
+ He guides me in the paths of righteousness
+ For His name's sake
+ Even though I walk through the valley of the shadow of death
+ I fear no evil
+ Thou art with me
+ Thy rod and thy staff, they comfort me
+ Thou dost prepare a table before me in the presence of my enemies
+ Thou has anointed my head with oil
+ My cup overflows

- Surely goodness and mercy will follow me all the days of my life

  And I will dwell in the house of the Lord forever.

GETTING INTO ALIGNMENT

I encourage you to start each day with a spiritual alignment. I have been doing this simple alignment exercise for years.

Just as fertile soil, with all the proper elements, provides the right environment for peak fruitfulness, so does the proper alignment of our spirit, soul and body provide the best environment for peak fruitfulness of the words we speak.

Here is the simple exercise I use:

> "I speak to my spirit: Arise, take your proper position, be the head of my being,
>
> Arise, spirit, and submit to the Holy Spirit.
>
> I speak to my soul – my mind, my will and my emotions: submit to my spirit, in proper Kingdom alignment.
>
> I speak to my body: submit to my spirit, come into proper Kingdom health and alignment.
>
> In the Name of Jesus."

Whenever I do this, I can actually feel a shift. It's awesome!

Do It! Live It! Be It!

The following pages contain Decrees inspired by select Psalms. Read them aloud. Command them over your life and over the lives of those in your household. Claim them for your businesses. As you do:

1. Order God's purposes and promises over yourself as with the authority of a Court Order;

2. Speak with the knowledge that the enemy is being cut off and his plans are being ripped off your life;

3. Renew your mind with truths about the presence and influence of the Lord in your daily life;

4. Watch the Kingdom of God manifest in your heart, your home and your life, for this is our truest prayer: "Thy Kingdom come, Thy will be done, on earth as it is in heaven."

DECREES *Inspired* BY THE PSALMS

1

I Am Blessed

Decree *Inspired* by Psalm 1

I am so blessed.

I am blessed when I walk, when I stand and when I sit down. I am blessed when I am about my work, when I take a moment to pause, and when I put my feet up to rest.

I am blessed when I am about my work because I do not plan my ways according to the counsel of the wicked. When I pause to contemplate, I do not think about the ways of sin or consider its fruit beneficial. When I rest, I do not let my mind wander to sarcasm or making fun of others.

Instead, I walk in the ways of the Lord, governed by the fruits of His Spirit. I sit and contemplate the ways of godliness and relax in love.

My delight is in the guiding ways and instruction of the Lord, and in His law I meditate both day and night.

I am like a tree planted firmly by streams of water, I am strong and well fed. I yield my fruit in season, my businesses do not fail, and I do not suffer miscarriage in health or in justice. My leaves do not wither but are healthy year round.

I prosper in all that I do.

The Lord knows my ways, for my ways are His ways. I am the righteousness of Christ. I will never perish, nor will my descendants or our inheritance.

2

HEAVENLY PERSPECTIVE

DECREE *Inspired* BY PSALM 2

God is my Father. I am His heir.
He sits in the heavenlies, at peace, His enemy conquered.
I am seated with Christ in the heavenlies, at peace, my
    enemies conquered.
I keep this mindset and heavenly perspective throughout my
    day.

God sits in the heavens and laughs!
He laughs at the antics of His conquered enemies
Because they are powerless before Him.
I sit with Him, confident in Him, and laugh at my enemies.

When the day seems set against me – not enough time, not
    enough sleep – I laugh.
The joy of the Lord is my strength.

When those I work with get into confusion and
    miscommunication, I laugh.
The favor of the Lord is my shield.
When my home is in uproar and emotions are raging, I
    laugh.
The love of the Lord covers a multitude of sins.

My way is sure and my path is clear because God's reign
    cannot be shaken.
God's plans for me are set – like the potter who molds the
    clay and
Then kilns it so that it sets and is firm – so is my life molded
    by Him,
Set and burning with the fire of His presence.

My heart is full of wonder for my God, whose enemies have
    been broken by Him.
I meditate on His might and His power and am filled with
    holy reverence for Him.
My whole being shakes with joy and fear, mixed together, as
    I contemplate His holiness.
With this God, I am safe and secure.
With this God, I can laugh at whatever comes my way.

My breath is the very breath of the living God.

3

Victory!

Decree *Inspired* by Psalm 3

I am protected. I am surrounded.
Jehovah holds my shield. Jehovah is my shield.

My head is lifted up above all my troubles.
I look down upon all the activities of my day and see that
    they are ordered.
Peace fills my soul.

I do not have to worry about defending my own name.
My reputation and dignity are kept safely in Jehovah-Kavod,
    who is the Lord of all Glory.
My glory and my honor belong entirely to Him.

All my prayers, cries and concerns are heard by Him.
All my prayers, cries and concerns are answered by Him.
He is faithful to me.

Those who are set against me are of no consequence to me!
I have no fear of them. The Lord sustains me.
I am revived and refreshed just by declaring His name.

Salvation, deliverance, welfare, prosperity, blessing, peace and
    victory
Have all been given to me as a gift from the Lord. They are
    mine.
I enjoy and possess them in every moment of the day.

4

VINDICATION FROM THE LORD

DECREE *Inspired* BY PSALM 7

The great thing about God is that I can trust Him.
His eternal plan protects me,
His friendship vindicates me,
His presence is my safe and calm retreat.

I am liberated from all the nonsense of the world's priorities.
He alone is my goal; I pursue Him for no reason other than
    to enjoy Him.

Jehovah, I give You the highest place of my heart!
You are established as the ruler over my family's generations.
You are set above. I ratify your promises over my household.

The justice of the Lord wins every time,
His justice is established over my life.
The rights and privileges of the Kingdom of Heaven are
   mine.

Deliverance, victory and prosperity are decreed for me.
He has set them in place and established them,
The time of breakthrough is now.

5

GODLY CHARACTER

DECREE *Inspired* BY PSALM 15

I choose God's character as my own: integrity, righteousness,
   truth.
These are like my backstage pass to God's personal tent.
Because of them, I can live with Him in holiness.

I take a stand against lies; I will not speak badly about others
   behind their backs and I will not be critical of my
   friends.
I choose to have soft eyes to see others.
I have a soft heart and understand that they, too, are on their
   journey.

I fear the Lord and honor others who do the same.

I am self-controlled and keep my emotions in check; I do not allow them to rule me.

I am accountable for my actions and take responsibility for myself.

I am quick to be generous. I love to give to others and do not expect anything in return.

I do not desire to profit from other people's loss.

Because I maintain a Godly character, I will never be shaken.

6

AT HOME AND AT PEACE
WITH THE LORD

DECREE *Inspired* BY THE 23RD PSALM

The Lord, the Creator of all things, the Divine One – He is
  my Protector!
He watches over me very carefully, with pleasure always in
  His eyes.
Everything that I need is already in His hands and He gives
  it to me lavishly!
My cupboards never run low, my gas tank is always full, I can
  tip generously.
My spirit soars throughout the entire day. My heart is never
  heavy.

I live in a relaxed state, calm and confident. His rest is always
new and fresh.
In the midst of the day I can close my eyes and feel the
coolness of His presence; He is my oasis.

When my mind is exhausted, He brings me back to my
strongest self,
When my patience is tried, He establishes His will in place
of my own,
When my integrity is tested, His ways always prove my
character.
Like currency at the Exchange, I receive strength and vitality
for my tiredness.

Even when my journey takes me through distress, danger or
dread,
My thoughts and emotions are stable.
I make absolutely no room for evil, misery or distress,
For the Lord Himself protects and avenges me.
His direction always leads me to safety.

The Lord establishes the details of my defense and
extinguishes all arguments against me.
He is the One to assess the value of my life.
Like the preparation of a royal banquet table, His care and
attention to details are focused for my benefit.
The Lord straightens, orders and organizes my life.

My head is anointed by the Lord. His anointing includes
blessings beyond compare, abundance, and prosperity.
My whole life overflows with His presence and His
goodness. His Spirit is life to me in all things.
My home and life overflow so much that I am able to really
enjoy sharing all that I have.

Goodness, favor, excellence, prosperity, happiness, kindness,
grace and beauty follow me and attend to me as my
helpers throughout all my life.

I will remain and be at home with the Lord always.

7

A Decree for the Media Mountain

Decree *Inspired* by Psalm 24

This Mountain is the Lord's!

This Media Mountain – all of its purposes were designed and built by God.

All those who dwell upon this Media Mountain are the Lord's.

We claim them for His righteousness.

We acknowledge the Olive Tree planted by the Lord atop this Mountain.

We declare that the anointing of the Lord dwells upon the Media Mountain.

We release His anointing, His purposes, His Spirit, and His Media.

We who love the Lord, who love His Media, we resolve to
ascend this Mountain!

Our faith is pure. With our hands we wield the power and
victory of the Most High.

Our mind is set on Christ. Our inner, secret self is sincere in
the pursuit of truth.

Our conscience and emotions are without compromise,
reflecting His pure light.

We are strong and full of courage.

We have the blessing of the Lord. His devotion is set toward
us.

He has lavished us with gifts upon gifts upon gifts – we
release them upon this Mountain.

The Lord has a peace treaty for the Media Mountain, His
desire is to restore the Mountain to its original intent
and purpose. We establish it for Him.

The time has come. We are the generation, the people, who
seek His face.

We are the dwelling place of the Most High.

We wrestle with the promise, we wrestle for the promise,

We set our hands and will not let go until this Media
Mountain is ours!

Hey! You portals of media, you gates of entryway, you
marketplace and public meeting places, you ancient
doors, you passageways of hope and you mouthpieces of
the heavens, we decree over you!

Be awakened, lift up your heads, open up, be released,
    receive a new blueprint and agenda, be restored to the
    foundation of your Creator and your purpose!

Make yourselves ready: the King of glory, of splendor, of
    dignity, honor and riches, He is ready to pass through.
The Lord of the angel armies, of all creation, the God of War
    is upon you.

8

How Great Is Your Goodness

Decree *Inspired* by Psalm 31

I trust the Lord. What a relief to know that I can.
I trust in His ways, in His promises and in His protection.
Because I trust in Him, I will never be ashamed!
I am delivered from my enemies. I am strong in
  righteousness.

The Lord listens closely and intently to me.
The answers I need come quickly, without interference or
  misunderstanding.
He takes time for me, there is no rush, I have all of His
  attention.
I conduct my life so that He alone is the force and influence
  around me.

I reside inside the place of the Lord, in His temple, in His heart.

There, no gossip, anger, bitterness, lies or revenge can reach me.

My household is secure. My children are saved.

Nothing that I own, or that is owed to me, can be taken from me.

Whatever the world tries to inflict on me is thwarted!

The words of God, the power of His love, the steadiness of His character,

They always provide a way for me, a way of escape and liberation.

Truth opens up the path, peace shows me how to go.

I have adopted God's thoughts and ways as my own.

With these as my tools for life, anything is possible!

My abilities are limitless, my future is open before me,

Nothing can hold me back or press me down. Nothing!

9

FORGIVEN

DECREE *Inspired* BY PSALM 32

I am absolutely privileged. I enjoy an advantage in life that
   others do not have:
My sins are forgiven and covered! It's as if they were never
   even committed.
I am humbled by the immense love that God has for me,
His forgiveness transforms my heart and life.

I enjoy this forgiven status, this special class with exclusive
   benefits.
Those who see the favor on my life are envious and are
   moved to seek God for themselves.

I am covered by the veil of God. He is careful with me, like a well-kept secret.

Instead of trouble surrounding me, I am surrounded by songs of jubilant escape:

I am safe, I am delivered, I am free!

I am secure. I pause to contemplate this truth.

My life is purposed for wisdom. All that I put my hand to is successful and prosperous.

I am the apple of God's eye and He never looks away from me.

I am transformed daily by the fresh mercy and gentle love of my Lord.

I am drunk with glee. I will not compromise my righteousness.

My determination, passion and courage are fixed because the Lord is mine.

10

I AM YOURS

DECREE *Inspired* BY PSALM 34:1–8

I live my life bowed on my knees before You, God, my King.
I bless You. You are the Eternal One.
I praise Your character. I intimately know Your glory.

In the private place of my heart, I adore You.
In the public place of my life, I show my gratitude.
From the depths of my being, I brag about You.

I am not shy about letting my life be an advertisement for
    You!
I am an encouragement to others to find themselves in You.

I take great care in seeking You and I know that You take
　　great joy in finding me.
You respond quickly to me and snatch me away from the
　　enemy's ploys.
I have no fears. I am completely at peace.

I look to You. I am never ashamed.
Your light transforms my heart so I can smile.
I beam with pride and joy – I am Yours.

My mind and spirit are in total awe of You because
I prosper in everything – everything that is ethical, excellent
　　and valuable.
My physical, social and financial state always continue to get
　　better and better!

11

EVERYTHING, ALWAYS

DECREE *Inspired* BY PSALM 34:9

I love the Lord. I choose His Kingdom.
I set myself apart from the world's ways.
I choose purity. I choose kindness. I choose being a good
person.

I don't care if I look old-fashioned and boring.
I don't care if I am laughed at.
I fear God. I am in awe of His power. I am in awe of His
humility.

Being snubbed by the world's system doesn't bother me at all,
Its definition of success is a façade, a complete fake.
The general attitude of having to "have it all" is empty and
worthless.

I have more than the world can offer me anyway.
Poverty is afraid of me and it runs away, escaping its own
    demise.
Lack and Need are terrified by what they see...

I live – completed.
Prosperity is mine and it multiplies in my hands.
Happiness increases constantly and is infectious to all who
    cross my path.
My soul thrives, my intellect and understanding are limitless.

All this abundance, all this goodness, has only one purpose
    in me –
To reflect the truth and light of the Holy One, my Rock.

12

ALL THAT I LONG FOR

DECREE *Inspired* BY PSALM 37

My trust is complete and satisfied in the Lord.
It is easy for me to think right thoughts and to choose
    suitable behavior,
I delight myself in the Lord, in the fullness of His majesty.
The attractions of the world have no influence over me.

I have committed every part of my day to Him,
I know I can trust God to bring me through successfully.
My reputation and credibility are protected and vindicated
    by God alone,
I cultivate my faithfulness with intention and purpose to
    know Him.

He gives me all that I long for:
The family I desire to have – children of strength, courage
and integrity,
The home I safeguard – full of peace and laughter and joy,
The walk with Him – resting under an open heaven.

I have inherited the land promised to me and to my
ancestors.
I choose humility every day and wear it like a garment,
And it is like spiritual currency that affords me abundance
and prosperity.
There is no room for anger, worry or irritation in my heart.

My enemies are cut off and the Lord laughs openly at them.
Their day has come, for they have been conquered.
The weapons they formed against me have been shattered.
I see this truth and am encouraged by the provision the Lord
has made for me.

I choose righteousness, and so the Lord sustains me,
My inheritance will stand forever.
I have no cause to be ashamed when opposition comes
against me,
For when the world suffers loss, I enjoy His mercy and
abundance.

DECREES

I love justice and run to it like a lifelong friend,
I constantly look for ways to be gracious and kind,
I close my ears from gossip and turn my eyes from impurity,
My mouth speaks the kindness of His heart.

The Lord will never leave me.
My life and my household are forever in Him.

13

STANDING TALL

DECREE *Inspired* BY PSALM 45

My heart is alive! I cannot even contain myself, I am so full
    of life!
Words of praise come spilling out of my mouth,
Like water tumbling over the falls.

God has blessed me, deeply and truly, He has undeniably
    blessed me!
He has given me words like honey to speak to my friends.
He has given me a fragrance like jasmine to attract His grace.
Finally, I see myself as He sees me and I am changed
    overnight.

I am standing tall, taller than I have ever stood.
Confidence is my new best friend.
I know no fear. I wear my armor with pride and with ease.

My sword is at my side, ready for striking.
My shield is raised and glistening in the light of His face.
A breastplate of righteousness guards my heart.
Truth, of who I am, of my strength and of my victory, keeps
    me on course.

My enemies lay all around, defeated, beaten, conquered.
They are at His feet, beneath His throne, silenced and still.
I stand before Him, covered by His blood, victorious.

I have a throne – it is His throne, glorious and pure.
I know the right way to live and I am living my best life ever.
I love honesty, integrity, sincerity and truth.
I put away drama and chaos and lies. I guard my peace.

The King has fallen head over heels in love with me,
He showers me with gifts day after day after day,
He has a procession of joy and laughter, and it surrounds me.

I set my mind toward the future, whatever it may hold.
My inheritance has been restored.
My children fill the earth and carry on this legacy of love.
We will remember the Lord and His goodness for
    generations to come.

14

RIGHT HAND

DECREE *Inspired* BY PSALM 63:8

Your right hand extends toward me,
You guide and direct me in the right way.
You keep me, according to Your Word, on the right path.

Christ is seated at the right hand of the Father.
I am in Christ and remain with Him, at the right hand,
The Father welcomes me to join Him and to sit at His right
hand.

All of the Father's Kingdom is at my right hand, within
reach—
Full of aid and comfort, complete with victory and strength.

Victory, strength, honor, wealth, riches and success,
All of these are mine, they are in Your right hand,
They are at my right hand.

15

HOW BLESSED

DECREE *Inspired* BY PSALM 65:4

Wow! You, God, Maker of the Universe, have chosen me.

I have been tested, I have been searched.
I have been examined as through a microscope
And I have been found pure, spotless, shining.

You position Yourself above and around me.
You draw in close, to hold and protect me.
Your embrace holds me, gently and tenderly.

My excellence is high above all others,
I have been selected as the preferred one,
My attributes bring the Lord joy and pleasure.

16

Inhabit Me, Oh Lord

Decree *Inspired* by Psalm 66:8–13

I bless You, Lord.

I set this time aside specifically to remember You and all that
You have done.

I make a point to tell others of Your faithfulness.

I am overwhelmed by You.

I am set in place by my Creator.

I have been painstakingly and carefully placed exactly in this
place.

I have authority over it; I rule over my household with the
fear of the Lord.

He tolerates nothing that prevents or impedes my strength
and stability.

I am sure in Him, in all things, in all places, in all
circumstances.

I am refined as silver,

As beautiful, precious, perfect, pure, solid silver.

Like a lover who carefully washes his bride – bathing her
and making her beautiful;

I have been prepared by the Lord.

I am prepared for my Lord to inhabit me as His dwelling
place.

Inhabit me, oh Lord. Completely and totally, take me over.

The Lord has caused me to be brought into His castle, into
His presence.

You, Lord, have brought about the pressure of labor pains,

I am the seat of all You have promised to bring to bear and
to pass.

You have strengthened me there in that place of labor and
have delivered me.

I am at peace – satisfied and complete in all that we have
promised to each other: I am Yours and You are mine.

17

HIS FACE SHINES

DECREE *Inspired* BY PSALM 67

God is merciful to me.
His grace surrounds me.
His favor restores me.
His face lights up with joy and
Shines upon my entire household.

The Lord shows me where to go,
I recognize His voice when He speaks
I am directed by His moral character,
His path leads me to safety and
In Him is my prosperity and victory.

18

JUST A GLIMPSE OF YOU

DECREE *Inspired* BY PSALM 84

From the innermost place of myself,
I am determined to seek the Lord.
From the part of my soul that lays awake at night

I crave His most intimate presence.
My heart, emotions and even my physical body
Sing with joy, inviting the King to overcome me.

This new happiness I have found –
It is clean, washed from the waterfall of His joy.
It makes even my thoughts shine and be pure.

The strength of person and conviction
Released upon me from His high tower
Brings resilience and conquers all fear.

Even when I pass through seasons of tears,
They create a deep well of life within me –
A source of growth, life and blessing.

Because of this, I know
That just a glimpse of Your goodness
Can last me a lifetime.

You are the Light, powerful and immense,
Standing as a prince over His betrothed,
Defending me against the world, against time.

There is nothing that You will keep from me,
Nothing that You will withhold or take away.
It is Your favorite joy to bless me.

You signed the title over to me, life is mine to enjoy.
I am completely accepted and enjoyed by You.
Every day, You are extravagant in Your gifts for me.

I can live in complete abandon toward You,
Completely unrestrained in my love and devotion for You,
Because I am that safe and secure in the place You've made
for me.

19

PROTECTION

DECREE *Inspired* BY PSALM 91

Ahhh, to rest. To sit in the Lord's presence, to relax in His beauty, to trust His strength. This is how I spend my nights!

I declare that the Lord God, who is above all things, is my home base, my safe place. I remember the childhood games where "home" was the safe place and no one could touch you while there. As I go through all the "games" of my day, I declare the Lord is my safe place. My trust and my confidence are absolute in Him.

I am rescued from surprises and protected from hazards. I am entirely safe, because Jesus fends off all danger. When traffic is hectic, I am safe. When co-workers are devious, I am protected. Whether traps or dangers are known to me or not, I am confident and fear absolutely nothing.

Others may suffer, but I do not have to. I expect the complete favor of God because He holds nothing back from me. His love is not conditional. His protection extravagantly surrounds me. I cannot even be grazed by danger. It's as if I am watching from a long distance away where nothing can reach me. I am bold in my expectation of comfort, happiness and security.

I declare that I am not intimidated. The Lord Himself has ordered His angels to stand guard over me wherever I go. If I stumble, they will catch me because it is their job to keep me from harm. Angels, do your job.

I hang onto Jesus with everything I've got. I know beyond the shadow of a doubt that He can and will get me out of any trouble. I receive the best possible care when I rest and trust Him completely.

Jehovah decrees over me, "*Call on Me and I will answer you. I will rush to you and remain at your side through all the ups and downs. I'll celebrate you with festivities and give you a long life, a long drink of my provision.*"

So I call upon the Lord, knowing that He has already answered me. Jesus has rushed to my side and remains with me through it all.

I am celebrated with festivals of pure joy. I enjoy my long, rich, full, blessed, honored life. And so it will be forever.

20

THE LORD IS BEFORE ME

DECREE *Inspired* BY PSALM 102

The Lord is ever before me. He hears my cry, He knows my voice. He listens for me with answers ready.

God reclines on His throne, in my heart and at home with me. The cherubim attend to Him. Their company, the angels and the Lord, quietly bring rest to my soul.

My days and my troubles, as difficult as they may seem, are really just fleeting moments before the eternity of the Most High, whom I love and in whom I am secure.

21

THE LIGHT OF GOD

DECREE *Inspired* BY PSALM 112:1–5

Jehovah's light upon my life guides me like the powerful
  intensity of a lighthouse.
Like the brilliance of the perfect diamond, His love is the
  radiance within me,
Brightening my heart and clearing my mind, I love the
  instruction of the Lord.

My entire household is full of extraordinary happiness,
  overflowing with the blessings of God, because I am in
  awe of Him.
I embrace the Lord's code of wisdom and make His ways
  mine.

People who know me rely on my strong moral character.

My children's character shines with honesty, modesty and
respectfulness.

A picture of my life would have me bowed on my knees
before the King,

He knights me with the sword of His Spirit and I rise before
Him,

Completely given over to serve His Kingdom.

It is easy for those in my family to generate wealth.

We all enjoy a special ability to create and maintain
substantial riches.

Our businesses, our passions and even our hobbies are
blessed.

Appraisers are always shocked at the high, inherent value of
all we have.

The legacy of my faith throughout my life will remain, and
take root in my children, grandchildren and great-
grandchildren.

Our family shield declares: truthfulness, excellence and
prosperity.

We remain firm and unwavering in our purpose, loyalty and
resolve to our King.

The light of God's fire burns up the darkness around me,

The light of God's instruction clarifies and purifies my soul,

The light of God's opulence and riches brings me joy – like
lights on a Christmas tree.

All that I am: my inner being of soul, my reason and resolve,
my conscience and determination, my heart and spirit,
are flooded by His brilliant light.

I shine, refreshed and rested.

22

A Right Attitude

Decree *Inspired* by Psalm 112:5–7

I have made graciousness and consideration of others my
   natural attitude.

My words are straightforward and just,
My actions are fitting and proper for a child of the King,
My heart is full of desire to please the Lord alone.
And because of this, my life is level – a straightened path.

Each morning I choose a friendly, generous attitude.
I understand that I don't always know what other people are
   enduring,
So my first reaction is always to offer them the advantage,
I adopt an attitude that honors others and willingly serves
   their needs above my own.

I am careful with my words and actions. I consider each situation carefully and gauge what is proper and fitting in each circumstance for business, work and home.

I have prepared my mind for the day. I set aside selfish motivations.

I am confident and content, without a care.

The Lord is my muse and inspiration.

My mind is renewed by His Spirit and presence.

23

THE DAY THE LORD MADE

DECREE *Inspired* BY PSALM 118:24–29

I dance around madly, as if no one is watching.
Complete joy and ecstasy are mine,
All because God is with me. He has made this day
And I know that His purposes will be completed in it.

Before I was born, God fashioned this very day;
He took care and purpose to shape it just for me.
I will conduct myself knowing today is ordained by God.
Today is reason enough to celebrate my life.

Today is the day I enjoy my liberation!
Victory, freedom, deliverance.
Who can fathom God giving aid to man?
I cannot, but I receive it with open arms anyway!

There is no end to the blessings of today.

I am happy, I am prosperous, my moral character is sure.

God's devotion to me is evident in today's new mercies.

I am overwhelmed by how rich His love is for me.

24

LIFE – GOD'S WAY

DECREE *Inspired* BY PSALM 119:32–40

I live my life the way God suggests and I see it suddenly
    expanding!
My future stretches out before me like the perfect
    countryside –
It's all pastureland, green fields and gently flowing rivers.

The journey my life course is set on is the roadway to His
    Kingdom.
I know that staying on this path only leads to one place:
Peace with God, peace of mind, and a clear conscience.

I chose this road for a reason, and I am determined to stay
    on it.
It's an ancient path, a steady and well-traveled way
That has never failed those who walk along its course.

I've come to love this pathway.

I feel life vibrating within me when I stay right in the middle.

It's like being gently shaken on a sifter — all the harshness of myself

Separates away, while all that is pure and fine collects together.

When the path turns, I follow. When it continues straight, so do I.

Because of this my heart remains naturally inclined to obey God.

Instinctively, I avoid and shy away from dishonest gain.

I look away from things that only appeal to my vanity and ego.

There is life and breath and freshness in all of God's ways,

And I embrace them with joy and committed passion.

God has set up traffic detours for everything that would derail me,

Long before I even get there, shame and disgrace are channeled far away.

This journey of life that I walk each day is good.

25

SECURE

DECREE *Inspired* BY PSALM 125

I am confident and secure in You, oh Lord,
My confidence is so sure that I am totally fearless before You!
I know my place in You – I am your highly favored one,
I can ask anything of You and I come into Your throne room
    every day.

You regard and keep me as Your sacred place, Your Mount
    Zion –
The place where Your chosen bride dwells and waits on You.
I am immovable. In You, I cannot shake, slip or fall.
I am intrepid – unwavering, courageous and brave.

You are my Jehovah – the One eternally existing,
    unchanging.

Forever You surround me, encircling me, doubling up round
and round.
Until the end of the age Your faithfulness to me is sure,
For you are eternal, timeless and faithful.

Regardless of the actions and behavior of others,
Whether they are ignorant, rebellious or cruel,
I shall not be compromised in my devotion to the ways of
God,
For I hold the scepter of the Lord, I uphold a standard
higher than theirs.

I am Your delight, Jehovah – I declare it from the
mountaintops!
In Your eyes I am beautiful and so much fun to be around.
Like the medicine of laughter, I am the joy in Your day.
I run to You in the Spirit; in the cool of the day, I am Yours
to enjoy.

Your thoughts and actions toward me are full of favor.
I am the beneficiary of all that is in You, of all that is good.
You lavish Yourself upon me, You lavish me with the
treasures of heaven
For in the deepest place of myself, I have chosen to live in
purity.

I decree peace, prosperity and contentment upon my life.
I decree them upon my children, my home and my extended
    family,
My co-workers, my work, my day, and all who cross my path.
The blessing of the Lord fulfills all my dreams and vision for
    life.

26

Rest and Provision, Even in Sleep

Decree *Inspired* by Psalm 127

I do not labor in vain; all I work toward is stable and sure.
The house I build is the Lord's.
He planned it and has kept it for me from the beginning.

I follow the Lord's leading, working alongside Him,
    cooperating with His Spirit.

I get up early in joy, and with gratitude
I eat the fruit of rest; I feast on peace.
I sleep calmly and peacefully all night long.

The Lord delights in sharing His abundance with me.
He fills my cupboards; He overflows my storehouse.
I am His pride and joy; He withholds nothing from me.

All this, while I sleep the deep, peaceful sleep of one in the
arms of love.

27

ALWAYS MORE, ALWAYS HIGHER

DECREE *Inspired* BY PSALM 128

Arise! Arise, thoughts of God's goodness! Arise, words of
   adoration!
For the Lord has set aside blessings and immense joy for me:

   I am careful with my day and with my time,
   I am careful with the presence of the Lord,
   I choose words and actions and moods that are
      inviting to Him.

   My life is a journey, and I love the adventure.
   I make my way through each day following His lead.
   I reap joy in every moment because I smile at every
      task.

I cannot stop laughing, and my days are filled with
    great friends
Because I avoid gossip and unkindness and don't
    cause others anxiety.
If there is anger, I calm it; if there is sadness, I ease it
    with care.

My family is my pride and joy, and I love to be with
    them.
The food in my house multiplies, and my supplies
    never diminish.
There is always so much to go around, we cannot stop
    giving it away.

My children shine from within, holy, pure and
    righteous;
They bring their stories to dinner and we feast
    together as friends.
They tell me of their dreams and passion, sharing
    their lives with me.

The Lord has blessed me and continues to bless me more
    every day!
My life is filled with beauty, joy, prosperity, property, riches,
    and gladness.

Always more, always higher, always increasing in all that I am,
The peace of lazy, warm summer days is mine every day,
And so it will always be.

28

LIFE IS GOOD

DECREE *Inspired* BY PSALM 144

I am blessed of the Lord. I say it again with passion:
I am blessed of the Lord!

And I bless the Lord, I bow before Him for He is great and
mighty.
My strength, which fuels the momentum of my
breakthrough, is from the Lord.
The Lord's sword and arrows are mine; He wields them in my
defense.

The Lord's salvation is so beautiful and His protection so
sure,
I cannot help but sing.

My children are strong and beautiful,
They are promoted in all they put their hands to.
My friends are many and they bear me up.
I am multiplied beyond the borders of my home.

I cannot contain my happiness for all I have in Him!

29

BLESS THE LORD

DECREE *Inspired* BY PSALM 145

I bless the Lord. I praise His greatness. I declare His
   faithfulness.
I am grateful beyond measure, and my words are changing
   the atmosphere;
I am creating an open heaven, with the intent and purpose to
   live there.
Great is the Lord and greatly to be praised.

   God is the head of this home,
   His ways are my ways,
   I put Him on the throne of my heart
   And lift up His faithfulness for everyone to see.

I yield to the Lord;
I bow before Him in holiness.

God's Spirit is within me,
His light shines with incomparable brilliance.
My mind is illuminated from within;
My soul is re-made by His clarity and purity.

The Lord's size is beyond measure,
His presence – intense beyond bearing.
His majesty and beauty cannot be fully known,
And yet…

I embrace Him and He engulfs me.

30

UNLIMITED!

DECREE *Inspired* BY PSALM 146

I unleash my praise to the Lord.
I radiate His Spirit beaming from within me,
I boast in His favor,
I cannot help but sing to Him all day, every day!

I do not rely on the generosity of others,
I do not find security in the world or in men,
They cannot help me.
My hope and provision come from the Lord.
I am so blessed in the riches of God,
He alone is my source.

I can afford to be ridiculously happy because
The One who made heaven and earth is my hope.
His size and greatness and abilities are unlimited.

Therefore, my abilities are unlimited because He is in me.
His strength never fails, which means my strength never fails.

These things are true:

> God is faithful, He is faithful to me.
> Justice is mine.
> I am never hungry, I am always full.
> I am never trapped, I am free.
>
> My eyes are open.
> I am raised up,
> I am loved,
> I am protected.
> I am supported and provided for.
> The wicked around me are thwarted before they even
>   begin.

31

His Goodness Invades

Decree *Inspired* by Psalm 147

My heart is transparent, my soul is clear like glass;
My spirit floats like a feather on the air.
The sound of my voice cuts the atmosphere like a trumpet
As I declare God's goodness.

I enjoy setting aside time to dwell on the beauty and
goodness of God.
The air is light and fresh. I can taste His presence like
misting rain.
I am completely preoccupied with Him.

The Lord provides permanent provision, restoring my hope
and my glory.

My inner man is healed and at peace,

Favor is restored to my home and family,

My businesses thrive, because the Lord builds them up.

My extended family and circle of personal friends are
encouraged.

His goodness invades every moment, every circumstance,
with laughter.

DECREES *Inspired* BY

THE PSALMIC

HEBREW LANGUAGE

1

LIGHT AND WAY

DECREE *Inspired* BY THE HEBREW WORDS 'OWR & DEREK AS USED IN JOB 22:28

I decree God's Light over myself:

> The light that shines brightly like the sun,
> The light that softens the darkness like the moon,
> The light that brings hope like the dawn,
> The light that brings warmth like a burning fire.
>
> I decree that the light of God's life is my life.
> The light of His instruction is my guide,
> The light of His prosperity is my friend, and that
> The light of His face shines over me.

His light exposes lies and restores truth in my defense.

His light encourages righteousness among all who
walk with me.

His light brings justice rendered in my favor.

I decree this light shines upon my way:

The journey of life that I travel,
That ancient pathway of God.

The moral character deep within that leads my steps,
my mannerisms, habits, and way of being.

2

TO JUDGE

DECREE *Inspired* BY
THE HEBREW WORD *SHAPHAT*
AS USED IN PSALM 7:11

I decree God as Judge over my life:

> He is my vindication, my reputation,
> The Judge of my life.
> His government is established over me.
>
> He decides the controversies,
> He executes the judgment on my behalf,
> He judges and punishes; I do not.

He defends my cause
And enters a judgment in my favor,
Delivering me from all who oppose.

His laws contend on my behalf,
And His government brings me peace.

3

INHERITANCE

DECREE *Inspired* BY THE HEBREW WORD *NACHALAH* AS USED IN PSALM 2:8

I claim the full, redeemed inheritance of my bloodline,
I claim the full and complete inheritance I have in Christ.
I claim it for myself, my family, my children and my
  children's children.
I claim it for generations to come:

> The earth is the Lord's and all it contains;
> He has transferred the dominion and authority over
>   to me.

> All blessings in heavenly places are given to me.
> The Promised Land is mine!

I take possession of the promises of God,
I possess and inhabit the land given to me,
I enjoy all the rights and privileges legally mine,
The heritage of the Lord is at my disposal.

I claim the property as my portion, my cup, my share.
The harvest is mine.

I am also the inheritance of Christ,
He possesses and inhabits me as His very own.
I am His prized possession, passed down to Him, a
gift from His Father.

4

PEACE

DECREE *Inspired* BY
THE HEBREW WORD *SHALOWM*
AS USED IN PSALM 125:5

I decree peace. I make way for peace.

Like a lava tube carved out of rock by the molten lava,
I declare that peace carves out the hard places of my heart
and makes way for the liquid fire and presence of God.

His peace completes me.
Peace makes my mind sound and my soul to prosper.
Peace creates for me a safe place, a refuge from the world.

My home is a place of tranquility and contentment;
Even though it may be busy, it is a place of rest.
My friends are at ease with me, we enjoy our time together.

My domain and sphere of influence are no longer at war,
But prosper in all things, rooted in peace.
I am at peace with God.

5

INCREASE

DECREE *Inspired* BY THE HEBREW WORD *YEBUWL* AS USED IN PSALM 67:6

"I praise the Lord, and the earth yields its increase to me."
This is a promise!

Therefore I praise the Lord:
I praise the Lord in the morning and in the evening.
I praise the Lord when I cannot see His way clearly.
I praise Him when He makes the way known.

Without hesitation and without question
I praise the Lord!

And I am given increase upon increase!
Watch and see how increase overtakes me.

The earth is the Lord's and all it contains.
The earth yields its increase to me by the decree of the
Lord!

The whole earth and all it contains
The land, the soil and waterways – yield your increase
for me.

My home upon the earth, my sphere of influence and
family friends,
Be fruitful, multiply, and yield all your goodness for
me.

My business, hobbies and new opportunities,
I decree increase!

Lost wages – repaid

Stolen time – restored

Sales and exchanges – growing

Work and business – profitable

Interest and dividend reports – rising

New ideas and inventions – downloaded

I speak to the riches of the earth: gold, oil, minerals
and gemstones,
Increase in value, increase in my portfolio, appear in
my midst.

I speak to the resources of the earth: water, air and
soil,
Increase in purity and in abundance, increase as my
possessions.

I decree the restoration of the earth,
I break the power of the curse and speak freedom!

I speak to the fruit trees and to the seeds planted by
the farmer:
Grow, prosper, free of insect and germ, full of life and
life-giving power.

I decree nourishment to the earth and welcome
nourishment in return.

I praise the Lord, for all that He does for me.
I praise the Lord for the increase granted to me.

Decrees for the 7 Mountains

Inspired by Psalm 24

7 Mountains

As Identified by Dr. Lance Wallnau

The 7 Mountains are a way of describing the seven most influential arenas that shape culture. The 7 Mountains could also be described as the seats of power that exist within the earth. They are:

1. The Business Mountain
2. The Government Mountain
3. The Family Mountain
4. The Religion Mountain
5. The Media Mountain
6. The Education Mountain
7. The Entertainment Mountain

The principles each Mountain represents speaks to a particular "mind-molder" in the sense that there is a way of thinking and operating that so deeply affects people groups that entire nations can shift with a perspective or belief. We see this when laws are enacted and when hit movies or bestselling books perpetuate a new philosophy.

Each of these Mountains has been dominated by forces and mindsets that are opposed to the Kingdom of God. But each Mountain was made by God for His purposes. God has destinies set aside for believers who are willing to ascend them and take them back.

1

A Decree for
the Business Mountain

Inspired by Psalm 24

This Mountain is the Lord's!

This Business Mountain – all of its purposes were designed
and built by God.

All those who dwell upon this Marketplace Mountain are
the Lord's.

We claim them for His righteousness.

We acknowledge the Olive Tree planted by the Lord atop
this Mountain;

We declare the anointing of the Lord dwells upon the
Business Mountain.

We release His anointing, His purposes, His Spirit, His
business, His increase,

His prosperity, His blessing, favor and grace.

We who love the Lord, who love being about the Father's
business,

We resolve to ascend this Business Mountain!

Our faith is pure. Our mind is set on Christ.

With our hands we wield the power and victory of the Most
High.

We declare that we cannot be bought or sold.

Our inner, secret self is sincere in the pursuit of honesty,
integrity and righteousness.

Our conscience and emotions are without compromise,
reflecting His pure light.

We are strong and full of courage.

We have the blessing of the Lord. His devotion is set toward
us.

He has lavished us with gifts upon gifts upon gifts – we
release them upon this Mountain.

The Lord has a peace treaty for the Business Mountain. His
desire is to restore the Mountain to its original intent
and purpose. We establish it for Him.

The time has come. We are the generation, the people who
seek His face.

We are the dwelling place of the Most High. We wrestle
with the promise, we wrestle for the promise, we set our
hands and will not let go until this Business Mountain
is ours!

Hey! You portals of business, inventions, strategies and
blueprints, you gates of entryway, you marketplace
and public meeting places, you ancient doors, you
passageways of hope and you mouthpieces of the
heavens, we decree over you! Be awakened, lift up your
heads, open up, be released, receive a new blueprint
and agenda, receive the heart of the Father and His
business; be restored to the foundation of your Creator
and your purpose!

Make yourselves ready: the King of glory, of splendor, of
dignity, honor and riches, He is ready to pass through.
The Lord of the angel armies, of all creation, the God of
War is upon you.

2

A Decree for the Government Mountain

Inspired by Psalm 24

This Mountain is the Lord's!

This Government Mountain – all of its purposes were designed and built by God.

All those who dwell upon this Government Mountain are the Lord's.

We claim them for His righteousness.

We acknowledge the Olive Tree planted by the Lord atop this Mountain;

We declare the anointing of the Lord dwells upon the Government Mountain.

We release His anointing, His purposes, His Spirit and His government.

We who love the Lord, who love His government, order and
authority,
We resolve to ascend this Government Mountain!
Our faith is pure. Our mind is set on Christ.
With our hands we wield the power and victory of the Most
High.

We declare that we cannot be bought or sold. We are not
vulnerable to lobbying.
Our inner, secret self is sincere in the pursuit of right
government, right rule.
Our conscience and emotions are without compromise,
reflecting His pure light.
We are strong and full of courage.

We have the blessing of the Lord. His devotion is set toward
us.
He has lavished us with gifts upon gifts upon gifts – we
release them upon this Mountain.
The Lord has a peace treaty for the Government Mountain.
His desire is to restore the Mountain to its original
intent and purpose. We establish it for Him.

The time has come. We are the generation, the people who
seek His face.
We are the dwelling place of the Most High. We wrestle
with the promise, we wrestle for the promise, we set
our hands and will not let go until this Government
Mountain is ours!

Hey! You portals of authority, leadership, rule and
government, you gates of entryway, you law forums
and public meeting places, you ancient doors, you
passageways of hope and you mouthpieces of the
heavens, we decree over you! Be awakened, lift up your
heads, open up, be released, receive a new blueprint and
agenda, receive Spirit-led leadership, be restored to the
foundation of your Creator and your purpose!

Make yourselves ready: the King of glory, of splendor, of
dignity, honor and riches, He is ready to pass through.
The Lord of the angel armies, of all creation, the God of
War is upon you.

3

A Decree for the Family Mountain

Inspired by Psalm 24

This Mountain is the Lord's!

This Family Mountain – all of its purposes were designed
and built by God.

All those who dwell upon this Family Mountain are the
Lord's.

We claim them for His righteousness.

We acknowledge the Olive Tree planted by the Lord atop
this Mountain;

We speak life, liberty, fruitfulness and eternity to this Tree.

We declare the anointing of the Lord dwells upon the Family
Mountain.

We release His anointing, His purposes and His Spirit.
We release His Love, His unity, His brotherhood and
    sisterhood.

We who love the Lord, who love being a part of the family of
    God,
We resolve to ascend this Family Mountain!
Our faith is pure. Our mind is set on Christ. We are one.
With our hands we wield the power and victory of the Most
    High.

We declare that we are for Christ, His family, His body. We
    are for unity.
Our inner, secret self is sincere in the pursuit of faith, hope
    and love.
Our conscience and emotions are steady, without
    competition or jealousy,
Reflecting His pure light. We are strong and full of courage.

We decree over this Mountain the fruit of the Spirit: love,
    joy, peace, patience,
Kindness, goodness, faithfulness, gentleness and self-control.
We decree the nature of love over the Family Mountain and
    over our families.
We decree patience and kindness. We cut off envy, boasting
    and striving.
We decree humility, and cut off rudeness and self-centered
    attitudes.

We make room only for righteous anger but keep no record of wrongs.

The Family Mountain rejoices in truth. We decree an atmosphere where

Love always protects, always trusts, always hopes, always believes the best.

Love perseveres. The Family Mountain is rich in the love that will never fail.

We have the blessing of the Lord. His devotion is set toward us.

He has lavished us with gifts upon gifts upon gifts – we release them upon this Mountain.

The Lord has a peace treaty for the Family Mountain, His desire is to restore the Mountain to its original intent and purpose. We establish it for Him.

The time has come. We are the generation, the people who seek His face.

We are the dwelling place of the Most High. We wrestle with the promise, we wrestle for the promise, we set our hands and will not let go until this Family Mountain is ours!

Hey! You portals of protection, you gateways of love, unity and intimacy, you covering places, you ancient doors, you passageways of hope and you mouthpieces of the heavens, we decree over you! Be awakened, lift up your heads, open up, be released, receive a new blueprint and agenda, be the thoroughfare of His peace, be restored to the foundation of your Creator and your purpose!

Make yourselves ready: the King of glory, of splendor, of dignity, honor and riches, He is ready to pass through. The Lord of the angel armies, of all creation, the God of War is upon you.

4

A Decree for the Religion Mountain

Inspired by Psalm 24

This Mountain is the Lord's!

This Religion Mountain – all of its purposes were designed
and built by God.

All those who dwell upon this sacred Mountain are the
Lord's.

We claim them for His righteousness.

We acknowledge the Olive Tree planted by the Lord atop
this Mountain;

We speak truth, purity, honesty, wise counsel and accuracy to
the Tree.

We declare the anointing of the Lord dwells upon the
Religion Mountain.

We release His anointing, His purposes and His Spirit. We
release Truth.

We decree the seven-fold Spirit of God over the Religion
Mountain:

The Spirit of the Fear of the Lord,

The Spirit of Wisdom and Knowledge,

The Spirit of Revelation and Prophecy,

The Spirit of Counsel and the Spirit of Truth,

The Spirit of Might and Power,

We decree the reign of the Holy Spirit!

We who love the Lord also love the widows and the orphans,
for this is true religion.

We resolve to ascend this Religion Mountain!

Our faith is pure. Our mind is set on Christ.

With our hands we wield the power and victory of the Most
High.

We declare that we will not be deceived.

Our inner, secret self is sincere in the pursuit of love, hope
and charity.

Our conscience and emotions are without compromise,
reflecting His pure light.

We are strong and full of courage.

We have the blessing of the Lord. His devotion is set toward
us.

He has lavished us with gifts upon gifts upon gifts – we
release them upon this Mountain.

The Lord has a peace treaty for the Religion Mountain. His
desire is to restore the Mountain to its original intent
and purpose. We establish it for Him.

The time has come. We are the generation, the people who
seek His face.

We are the dwelling place of the Most High. We wrestle
with the promise, we wrestle for the promise, we set our
hands and will not let go until this Religion Mountain
is ours!

Hey! You spirit portals, you gates of entryway, you sacred
and holy places, you ancient doors, you passageways
of truth and faith, you mouthpieces of the heavens,
we decree over you! Be awakened, lift up your heads,
open up, be released, receive a new blueprint and
agenda, receive truth, receive love and be restored to the
foundation of your Creator and your purpose!

Make yourselves ready: the King of glory, of splendor, of
dignity, honor and riches, He is ready to pass through.
The Lord of the angel armies, of all creation, the God of
War is upon you.

5

A DECREE FOR THE MEDIA MOUNTAIN

Inspired BY PSALM 24

This Mountain is the Lord's!

This Media Mountain – all of its purposes were designed and built by God.

All those who dwell upon this Media Mountain are the Lord's.

We claim them for His righteousness.

We acknowledge the Olive Tree planted by the Lord atop this Mountain;

We declare the anointing of the Lord dwells upon the Media Mountain.

We release His anointing, His purposes, His Spirit and His media.

We who love the Lord, who love His media, we resolve to
ascend this Mountain!

Our faith is pure. With our hands we wield the power and
victory of the Most High.

Our mind is set on Christ. Our inner, secret self is sincere in
the pursuit of truth.

Our conscience and emotions are without compromise,
reflecting His pure light.

We are strong and full of courage.

We have the blessing of the Lord. His devotion is set toward
us.

He has lavished us with gifts upon gifts upon gifts – we
release them upon this Mountain.

The Lord has a peace treaty for the Media Mountain; His
desire is to restore the Mountain to its original intent
and purpose. We establish it for Him.

The time has come. We are the generation, the people, who
seek His face.

We are the dwelling place of the Most High. We wrestle
with the promise, we wrestle for the promise, we set our
hands and will not let go until this Media Mountain is
ours!

Hey! You portals of media, you gates of entryway, you
marketplace and public meeting places, you ancient
doors, you passageways of hope and you mouthpieces
of the heavens, we decree over you! Be awakened, lift up

your heads, open up, be released, receive a new blueprint and agenda, be restored to the foundation of your Creator and your purpose!

Make yourselves ready: the King of glory, of splendor, of dignity, honor and riches, He is ready to pass through. The Lord of the angel armies, of all creation, the God of War is upon you.

6

A Decree for the Education Mountain

Inspired by Psalm 24

This Mountain is the Lord's!

This Education Mountain – all of its purposes were
designed and built by God.

All those who dwell upon this Mountain of knowledge and
inspiration are the Lord's.

We claim them for His righteousness.

We acknowledge the Olive Tree planted by the Lord atop
this Mountain;

We declare the anointing and peace of the Lord dwell upon
the Education Mountain.

We release His anointing, His purposes, His Spirit and His
education.

We speak the Wisdom of the Lord and the Knowledge of the Holy One.

We who love the Lord, who love His discipleship, we resolve to ascend this Mountain!
Our faith is pure. With our hands we wield the power and victory of the Most High.
Our mind is set on Christ.
Our inner, secret self is sincere in the pursuit of truth.
Our conscience and emotions are without compromise, reflecting His pure light.
We are strong and full of courage.

We have the blessing of the Lord. His devotion is set toward us.
He has lavished us with gifts upon gifts upon gifts – we release them upon this Mountain.
The Lord has a peace treaty for the Education Mountain; His desire is to restore the Mountain to its original intent and purpose. We establish it for Him.

The time has come. We are the generation, the people who seek His face.
We are the dwelling place of the Most High. We wrestle with the promise, we wrestle for the promise, we set our hands and will not let go until this Education Mountain is ours!

Hey! You portals of truth and learning, you gates of
entryway, you places of education and mentoring, you
portals of the agora and high places, you ancient doors,
you passageways of hope and you mouthpieces of the
heavens, we decree over you! Be awakened, lift up your
heads, open up, be released, be released from deception
and lies, be purified, be released of false agendas, receive
a new blueprint and agenda. We decree that only truth
can flow through you, we cut off deception, lies and the
wisdom of the world. We cut off questioning against
God's authority and truth. We decree the fear of the
Lord, His wisdom and understanding, his revelation
and prophecy. Education Mountain, be restored to the
foundation of your Creator and your purpose!

Make yourselves ready: the King of glory, of splendor, of
dignity, honor and riches, He is ready to pass through.
The Lord of the angel armies, of all creation, the God of
War is upon you.

7

A Decree for
the Entertainment Mountain

Inspired by Psalm 24

This Mountain is the Lord's!

This Entertainment Mountain – all of its purposes were
designed and built by God.

All those who dwell upon this Entertainment Mountain are
the Lord's;

We claim them for His righteousness.

We acknowledge the Olive Tree planted by the Lord atop
this Mountain.

We declare the anointing, peace and unity of the Lord dwells
upon the Entertainment Mountain.

We release His anointing, His purposes, His Spirit.

We decree His laughter, His joy, fun, and delight. We release
His entertainment.

We who love the Lord, who love His presence, we resolve to ascend this Mountain!

Our faith is pure. With our hands we wield the power and victory of the Most High.

Our mind is set on Christ. Our inner, secret self is sincere in the pursuit of purity.

Our conscience and emotions are without compromise, reflecting His delight.

We are strong and full of courage.

We have the blessing of the Lord. His devotion is set toward us.

He has lavished us with gifts upon gifts upon gifts – we release them upon this Mountain.

The Lord has a peace treaty for the Entertainment Mountain, His desire is to restore the Mountain to its original intent and purpose. We establish it for Him.

We speak purity and purification over the Entertainment Mountain.

We wash you with the Word of the Lord; We bless you in His Name.

We decree the restoration of the joy of the Lord, the pleasure and rest of God.

The time has come. We are the generation, the people who seek His face.

We are the dwelling place of the Most High.

We wrestle with the promise, we wrestle for the promise,

We set our hands and will not let go until this
Entertainment Mountain is ours!

Hey! You portals of entertainment, you gates of entryway,
you marketplace and public meeting places, you ancient
doors, you passageways of hope and you mouthpieces
of the heavens, we decree over you! Be awakened, lift up
your heads, open up, be released, receive a new blueprint
and agenda. We shut down portals of perversion, we
destroy wickedness, vulgarity and mammon. We destroy
the spirits that lure God's children into dark places and
secrecy.

We speak life and revelation over the portals of
entertainment! Receive joy, fun and laughter from the
Throne Room. Be purified, be invigorated and inspired,
be restored to the foundation of your Creator and your
purpose!

Make yourselves ready: the King of glory, of splendor, of
dignity, honor and riches, He is ready to pass through.
The Lord of the angel armies, of all creation, the God of
War is upon you.

To order more copies of *Decrees Inspired by the Psalms*, write:
info@WhiteQuillMedia.com

You will also find ordering information on:
www.Facebook.com/WhiteQuillMedia

You may order more copies of *Decrees Inspired by the Psalms* and other books from XP Publishing at the XPmedia.com store.

BULK ORDERS: We have bulk/wholesale prices for stores and ministries. Please contact: usaresource@xpmedia.com.

For Canadian bulk orders, contact: resource@xpmedia.com or call 250-765-9286.

XPpublishing.com

A ministry of Christian Services Association